Be the Chocolate Chip

By Jen Brewer, RD

with Amy Stucky

Published in the United States by:

PETERSEN

PRESS

Petersen Press
P.O. Box 6074
Rochester, MN 55903
Petersenpress.com

ISBN: 978-0-9835140-7-7
First Paperback Edition

To order a copy of this book, please visit: Bethechocolatechip.com

At the time of publication, all website addresses were verified as accurate.
The authors do not assume responsibility for updates, errors, or changes
in website content or addresses that occurred after publishing.

Acknowledgments:

Many thanks to the many hands that worked

to take this book from idea to publication.

The dear Rochester Mamas performed

collaborative editing magic.

David Cheney's cover art was spot on, and

Ryan Ledebuhr's designing eye could fix things

we never even knew needed fixing.

This Book is Dedicated to:

the amazing youth of

The Church of Jesus Christ

of Latter Day Saints.

Thank you for continually standing up,

standing strong, and staying firm.

TaBle of Contents

Chapter One

The Birth of the Chocolate Chip

In 1930, Ruth Wakefield and her husband owned an inn outside of Wakefield, Massachusetts. Built in 1709, the old house was used as a rest stop for travelers to change their horses, pay their tolls, and get something to eat, earning it the name "The Toll House Inn." The Wakefields kept the tradition of providing travelers with rest and good food through the Great Depression.

Ruth Wakefield was well known for her baking, and often made Butter Drop Do Cookies. Her recipe required baker's chocolate, which melted completely, producing a chocolate cookie. One day in 1937, as she began making the cookies, she realized she was out of baker's chocolate, but happened to have a nestle semi-sweet chocolate bar on hand. She chopped it into chunks and put it in the batter, expecting it to disappear and melt into the cookie, producing the familiar chocolate cookie for which she had grown famous.

To her surprise, the chocolate chunks did not disappear, but held their individual shape, producing a creamy texture and a fabulous new taste for the entire cookie.

These new cookies became incredibly popular. Nestle® bought the rights to the recipe, and in 1939 introduced Nestle Toll House Real Semi Sweet Chocolate Morsels®. The traditional "Chocolate Chip Cookie" was born!

The most popular cookie of all time came about all because a bit of chocolate held its ground and didn't melt when the heat was on.

You, too, can be the chocolate chip. Satan knows your potential. He is constantly trying to mix you into the world and get you to lose your individual worth. Satan knows how to turn up the heat. He thinks that if he does his job well you will melt under the pressure, get lost in the crowd, and lose your understanding of who you really are: a child of God.

He will try to make you think that you can only feel good about yourself if you become part of the world and do what "everyone else" is doing. But you can be like the wonderful chocolate chip. Christ talks about you in Doctrine & Covenants 132:16: *"They are not of the world, even as I am not of the world."*

You *can* be the chocolate chip. You can choose to be '*in* the cookie, but not *of* the cookie.' Just as the chocolate chip made the cookie better by retaining its true nature, you can make the world better by retaining your true nature as a follower of Christ. You don't have to be something or someone else. You don't have to melt into the crowd; you can be the chocolate chip! You will get noticed for being different. You will stand out. That is what makes all the difference, and is what makes a chocolate chip cookie so great. What good would it be without the chocolate chips? Be you. Be different. Be better.

Be the chocolate chip!

Be the Chocolate Chip... But how??

Like many things in life, knowing and doing are two different ball games. We all know that we should stand out and not get sucked into the crowd or give in to peer pressure. But it's a whole different story when we are standing face-to-face with our friends and you have to literally take a stand, sometimes even at the cost of the friendship.

Yes, it's hard.

Yes, it can be incredibly frustrating. At times it even feels like we are getting punished for trying to do the right thing. But we are not alone.

YOU are not alone. You have help. You have support.

Here are four ways that you can be the chocolate chip:

1. Covenants

2. Hold on

3. Individuality with Integrity

4. Personal Perfection

Chapter Two

covenants

Members of The Church of Jesus Christ of Latter-day Saints are a covenant-making people. Our very first step is our baptismal covenant. This helps us start fresh and new, and takes us to our first step in standing out. Elder Robert D. Hales stated in General Conference October 2000: "At baptism we make a covenant with our Heavenly Father that we are willing to come into His kingdom and keep His commandments from that time forward, even though we still live in the world."[1] Through baptism, we covenant with God that we will take His name upon us, that we will always remember Him. The very act of baptism helps us to stand apart. It is the outward ordinance that follows the inward conversion. Walking into the waters of baptism helps each of us take the first stride of stepping out of the world, and into the kingdom of God.

Throughout history, many people have taken this first step. For some it was simple and straightforward, as in the case of King Benjamin's people. They heard the teaching. They were touched by the spirit. The scriptures called this a mighty change of heart, even to the point that they *"had no more disposition to do evil, but to do good continually."* (Mosiah 5:2) They knew they needed to do something differ- ent from that point on, even to the end of their lives. For them it was a natural progression. Each person individually chose to enter into the waters of baptism.

A little later in the Book of Mormon, a similar group of people also had a change of heart. This group of people was few in number. Theirs was a world not of peace and harmony, but of great evil and discord. They lived in the time of King Noah. When they heard the teachings of Alma, however, the spirit was the same. They heard the teach- ing. They were each touched by the spirit. They knew they needed to be different. The scriptures tell us that they were willing to *"stand as a wit- ness of God at all times, and in all places."* (Mosiah 18:9) In order to follow their beliefs, this group of people had to literally stand up and stand out (as in flee!!) in order to fulfill the covenant of baptism. But they did it. Risking great peril in a crazy world, they entered into the waters of baptism. (Mosiah 18:16) They became the chocolate chips, standing steadfast and immovable in the ever-growing heat of the world.

In our time entering the waters of baptism and making this sacred covenant with God does not mean that we have to run and hide. In fact, it means just the opposite. Elder Hales taught us, "by choosing to be in His kingdom, we separate — not isolate —ourselves from the world. Our dress will be modest, our thoughts pure, our language clean. The movies and television we watch, the music we listen to, and the books, magazines, and newspapers we read will be uplifting. We will choose friends who encourage our eternal goals, and we will treat others with kindness. We will shun the vices of immorality, gambling, tobacco, liquor, and illicit drugs. Our Sunday activities will reflect the commandment of God to remember the Sabbath day and keep it holy. We will follow the example of Jesus Christ in the way we treat others. We will live to be worthy to enter the house of the Lord."[1]

As we proceed throughout life, we also make other covenants that help to strengthen us in our quest to stand strong and stand out. Inside the temple, we make New and Everlasting Covenants that seal us as families through the bonds of marriage not only in this life, but also past the claws of death, into eternity.

Think about that. Really stop and think about it for a moment. A God who loves us so perfectly, and knows the fiery trials that surround us on all sides, has made a way not only for us to stand strong through baptism, but to also have a companion by our side to walk with us through the perils of life on earth. Through our faithfulness to God and our spouse, a bond will be created that outlasts all of life's great destructive forces, even death. That is big-time Hollywood — Huge! Don't settle. Hold out for that amazing companion. And while you're waiting, work on *being* that amazing companion for him or her.

As we well know, covenants are not one-sided. We make covenants with God, and He, in turn, makes covenants with us; covenants that He is bound to keep as long as we hold up our end of the bargain (Doctrine & Covenants 82:10). Although God is bound to keep His covenant, it's a little trickier for us mortals! We live in a time where "keeping covenants" is not always the popular thing to do.

In the Book of Mormon, even the wicked understood the value of covenant keeping. The Lamanites were faced with a choice to make a covenant of peace, or die. The choice, as explained by Moroni was: (a)put down your weapons of war or (b) we will kill you (I love Moroni's explanation: *"inflict the wounds of death in your bodies that ye may become extinct."* [Alma 44:7] Now that's not mincing any words!).

The choice of the Lamanite leader was very interesting. He said they would put down their weapons, but they would *not* make an oath that they *knew they would break* (Alma 44:8). That is amazing. Even the wicked knew the importance of keeping a promise. At the expense of their own lives, they would not enter into a promise falsely. Look around you today. How is the value of a promise perceived in our society? Not very highly. But God expects us to keep our promises. And when we do, He will keep His part of the covenant with us.

Chapter Three

HolD on

(With the Help of the Holy Ghost)

God has promised that he will not leave us alone to fight the fight. As the baptismal covenant states, when we always remember Him, we will have His spirit to be with us (see 3 Nephi 18:7). This is in a very real sense. After baptism, we literally receive the gift of the Holy Ghost, an actual member of the Godhead! We can then claim hold on Him to help us stand strong and firm throughout our mortal journey.

Entering the waters of baptism is not the end. In fact, it is the opposite. It is the beginning of a journey into a new life. Nephi explained it perfectly when he was teaching his people about the journey of mortality. In 2 Nephi 31: 19-20, he taught the people that getting baptized was only the beginning — that there was much more to do. He admonished them to *"...press forward with a steadfastness in Christ, having a perfect brightness of hope, and a love of God and of all men."* He went on to say that if we do these things and *"feast on the words of Christ, and endure to the end, behold, thus saith the Father: we shall have eternal life."*

Unfortunately, the temptations of Satan do not end as we come up out of the waters of baptism. At times, it may even seem as if he doubles his efforts to get us to fail. President Gordon B. Hinckley, a prophet of God, warned the youth of the Church: "I say, be true. Hold to the faith. Stand firmly for what you know to be right. You face tremendous temptation. It comes at you in the halls of popular entertainment, on the Internet, in the movies, on television, in cheap literature, and in other ways — subtle, titillating, and difficult to resist. Peer pressure may be almost overpowering. But, my dear young friends, you must not give in. You must be strong. You must take the long look ahead rather than succumbing to the present seductive temptation."[2]

The pressure is there, and it is real. You will be tried and you will be tested. The heat will be turned up. But as we endure the furnace of the adversary, we are not alone. We have the Holy Ghost. And we must rely on the help of the Holy Ghost. God promises not to allow us to be tempted above that which we are able to bear. (D&C 64:20) God keeps his promises. We can be strong, we can hold on. With His help, we can hold out faithful until the very end.

So... hold on and hold strong! The path along the iron rod is not a casual stroll through the meadows of life. It requires us to steadfastly press forward through mists of darkness, *clinging* to the rod so as not to be lost in the mist, as many were — and still are. The account of the tree of life in 1 Nephi 8 gives a perfect explanation of how to hold strong. In fact, Nephi uses the word *"clinging"* to the iron rod. Many came and started on the path. But when times got tough, those who were not clinging were lost. Keep clinging, don't ever let go!

Our fifth child came after a succession of three boys. Being a loving mother, I worried a bit about her ability to withstand the pressures of her older brothers. One day, as one of her brothers made a bee-line for a toy she was holding, my worries were swept away. Her eyes changed and she became determined. She knew she was about to be challenged. I saw her tiny fingers turn into a vice around her precious possession. She ducked, and used her whole body as a shield to what she was holding. She knew it and I knew it: she was not going to let go of that toy. Eventually her brother (more than double her size) got the message and gave up his quest for the item.

I have thought about that experience many times since. How much do we prize the precious gift of the gospel? Do we hold on when the times get tough? Do we use our whole body to shield this precious gift in our grasp? Do we let go when the mists come up, or when something that seems more enticing beckons us to loosen our grip?

Companionship with the Spirit will give us the strength to resist evil and when necessary, repent and return to the strait and narrow path. None of us is immune from the temptations of the adversary. We all need the fortification available through the Holy Ghost.

Chapter Four

InDiviDuality With Integrity

We must stand apart from the world, but with integrity. Within the church, we are one in belief and purpose. But we are each still individuals, with personal and unique differences. If you ever peruse the baking aisle of the grocery store, you will find a vast variety of chocolate chips: milk chocolate, semi-sweet, white chocolate, mint, butterscotch, cinnamon, caramel, big, small, jumbo — just to name a few. They are all different. But they all have the same core characteristic: to stand strong and firm in the midst of the cookie.

So it is with us. We can use our individuality to create a strong unity within the gospel setting and help the Church to become an even stronger force for good in the world. James E. Faust stated: "All of us want to find out who we really are and what our place is in the world. Some of you young people are trying to find your identity by being different from your parents and families in what they stand for. God made each of us to be different from anyone else in the world, as our DNA and fingerprints prove. You don't have to work at having a separate identity; you already have one."[3]

You are different than anyone else on the planet. You are an individual. You don't have to be anyone but yourself. Find your core and be true to what you know is right. Stand up and stand strong.

But being individual will do little without the core of integrity. In short, integrity is "always doing what is right and good, regardless of the immediate consequences."[4] The true test of integrity and character come down to this question: What would you do if you knew you would never get caught?

Satan uses many tools. Among his most powerful is the Internet with its great mask of anonymity. He tries to melt you into the masses by telling you that no one really knows what you are doing. You are alone. You are behind a screen. Others only see your screen name, not your real name. He tries to twist and turn your values until they can become little more than a distant thought. As your values begin to fade, you may soon realize that your true nature is nowhere to be found. Your screen name will have taken precedence over your values and you can no longer distinguish yourself from the masses — in essence...you have melted.

Don't give in! Integrity is so much more than giving the right Sunday School answers in class each week. It is constantly keeping alive the thought that you truly are an offspring of God. You are part of Him. Every choice, every day can bring you closer to Him, or take you away from Him. Integrity is being true to the God-like nature that is inside of you.

Just think about the power that could be brought about if every young man and woman in the Church truly lived the standards, not just 'abided' by them when the adults were around. A story told by President David O. McKay in 1911 illustrates how the power of the Church body truly depends on the integrity of the individual: "I was with a party of friends recently, driving over a beautiful valley, not far from Salt Lake City. We passed a beautiful wheat field. It was an impressive sight really to see that dry farm of wheat, and one of the party expressed his admiration.... But he was not satisfied with looking at it in the aggregate; ... he looked at individual heads of wheat and exclaimed, 'Look what large heads.' ... He broke the head, shuffled it in his hand, blew the chaff away, and examined each kernel. 'The kernels,' continued he, 'are plump and solid.' After all, the test of that wheat field was the individual kernel of wheat, and so it is in a community, so

it is in the Church. The test, after all, of the effi-
ciency of God's people is an individual one. What
is the individual doing? Each one should ask, 'Am
I living so that I am keeping unspotted from the
evil of the world?' "5

God also talks of the power that is possible
if all people were 'as (the prophet) Mormon,'
who was filled with integrity. He states that
"the very powers of hell would have been shaken
forever; yea, the devil would never have power
over the hearts of the children of men." (Alma
48:17) He names people who fit that description:
Moroni, Ammon and his brothers, Helaman and
his brothers. "For they were all men of God."
(Alma 48:18) How would it feel to know that God
thought of you in that way? How would it feel to
have Satan say each day when you wake up (as
Sheri Dew submits), "Oh no! he/she's up again!"6

There is power in integrity. Power for good.
Power to not melt into the masses, but be numbered among the great ones. Take a look at your
life. Really look. Do your actions follow your
testimony? How is your testimony? Some of you
may be thinking, "she's talking about the 'good
ones,'" or "that's not me, I've messed up too much,
there's no hope for me to turn around now." If
those are your thoughts, read the following
paragraphs carefully:

When God listed by name the people who literally had the power to shake the powers of hell,

he named Ammon among those men. This is the same Ammon, who just a few chapters earlier had been numbered among the unbelievers (Mosiah 27:8-12, 16). He actually sought to destroy the church to the point that an angel was sent down from Heaven to stop him.

Still think you are beyond hope? Let's take Paul. Before Paul became Paul, he was known as Saul; a Jewish leader who hated Christians. More than simply preach against the gospel, he persecuted the believers of Christ. In fact, on one such journey to round up and imprison the believers of Christ, Jesus Himself stopped Saul. Then, even before Saul was baptized, the Lord called him a chosen vessel. (Acts 9:4-15). Saul saw the error of his ways. He repented, was baptized, and started a whole new life (with the new name of Paul). He became a great missionary and man of God. Paul truly stood strong and held his shape when the heat was on, never wavering, even to the end.

Whatever you have done in your life, there is a way back. If Ammon can go from the rebuke of an angel to a chosen man of God, and Paul can go from persecuting believers of the Gospel to preaching the Gospel, you can come back. Repent. Repair what needs to be repaired. Change what needs to be changed. You are not too far-gone to stand strong and stand firm.

Chapter Five

Personal Perfection

Perfection is a personal journey — no one can do it for us. It is not an easy road. We will be tried. We will be tested. It is one of the few things in life that is ours and ours alone.

Too often, we think of perfection as being without blemish; not having ever made one mistake. By that definition, everyone has already failed. There is no way we can make it through this life completely free of any blemish of the world.

Theodore M. Burton gave us a different idea about perfection. He taught: "I dare not say that Mormons are perfect, for you know as well as I do that we each have many human faults. We do, however, call ourselves saints as did the members of the Church of Jesus Christ in the days of the original apostles. When those apostles wrote letters to the members of the Church they addressed them as saints. A saint is not necessarily a person who is perfect, but he is a person who strives for perfection — one who tries to overcome those faults and failings that take him away from God. A true saint will seek to change his manner of living to conform more closely to the ways of the Lord."[7]

It is in the striving that we show God our commitment. We may look at where we are, and how far we have to go and get overwhelmed. It's easy to do, for there truly is so far for us to go.

Let me share this example: Have you ever seen a child attempting his first, timid, solo steps in the world? If you have the chance, I would urge you to not watch the child. Turn and watch the parent. There you will find the essence of our Heavenly Father as he watches us on our daily journey towards personal perfection. The parent knows that the child must take the step alone. The parent is there, ready to catch **when** — not if — the child falls. For the parent knows that the child will fall, perhaps many times, before their child becomes "perfect" in walking. Yet on the parent's face there is no anger that the child has not mastered the art of walking. If you look closely, you will see the purest form of unabashed love and joy. The parent claps for joy at each and every step. He or she doesn't scold or condemn the child for only taking two or three steps when the goal was ten, but rejoices that the child has taken three full steps! Then, each time the wobbly legs get a little stronger to last a few more steps, more rejoicing follows.

Perfection is not an act, it is a process. It is a process of thousands of tiny movements toward a single goal that, when performed with enough repetition, become part of our make-up. The commandments and counsel that we hear over *and over* and over again are there to help us practice over *and over* and over again the tiny, seemingly insignificant acts that will ultimately lead to our perfection. Through each stepping-stone, we will become more like our Savior and closer to exaltation. Eventually when we become perfect as He is, we will obtain all that he has and live out the remainder of eternity with our loved ones at our side.

Think about that! Is laying aside five, ten, or even thirty minutes a day too much to ask to build a habit of scripture study that will not only help us stay firm and unmelted, but will lead to our personal perfection and the opportunity to live with God and our families forever? Is forsaking some of the habits that we know are taking us away from God too much to ask in exchange for perfection?

Forever is a long time to live with "what could have been."

We don't have to be perfect today. We can't be perfect today. But we can be moving towards perfection everyday. God is there, though we can't physically see Him. He is there, with that same parental expression of joy and hope, cheering us on as we take our toddling steps toward total perfection.

Although perfection is an individual journey, none of us can get there by our merits alone. Each and every one of us requires help from Jesus Christ and His Atonement. In *Believing Christ*, Stephen Robinson compares the Atonement to a corporate merger: "Perfection comes through the Atonement of Jesus Christ. That happens as we become one with Him, a perfect being. It is like a merger. If you take a small, bankrupt firm that is about to go under and merge it with a corporate giant... their assets and liabilities flow together, and the new entity that is created is solvent. This is similar to what happens spiritually when we enter into a covenant with the Savior. We have liabilities; He has assets. So He proposes a covenant relationship... I become one with Christ... I do all that I can do, and He does what I cannot yet do. For now, in partnership we are perfect, through His perfection."[8]

Someone who really understood this perfect partnership with God and Jesus Christ was the brother of Jared. I love his faith. I love his fortitude. I love the whole story of building ships to cross the ocean recounted in Ether chapters two and three:

The brother of Jared comes to God with two concerns — the ships are so tight that there is no air or light (Ether 2:19). God, being the loving parent that He is, provides an outright answer to the concern about air. When the brother of Jared presses on, wanting the answer to the other dilemma (no light), God then begins to teach and test the brother of Jared, asking him what *he* would want God to do. The next part is what amazes me. The brother of Jared conceives a plan. It is a plan that requires a great amount of work on his part (molten rocks? That's hard work!). But the kicker in the plan is this: from the outset the brother of Jared knew that in order for his plan to come to fruition, it would literally require the Lord's hand. You know how the story unfolds (or if you don't, go read it in Ether chapters two and three — great story!).

Could we be so bold as to come up with plans in life that *require* the hand of God to see them through to completion? Many times we take one extreme or the other — either the "I'll do it myself!" approach, or the "It's too hard, I can't do anything" excuse. The true answer to obtaining perfection comes in following the blueprint of the brother of Jared: we work on all that is possible for us to work on, knowing full well that in the end, it will require the hand of Christ to complete perfection. So we go forward in faith, day in and day out, working out our perfection in any and all ways that we can. Then we rely on the merits of Christ to make up the difference (2 Nephi 31:19, 2 Nephi 25:24).

The road to perfection is going to get hot. Satan will try to melt us. But he is not the only one turning up the heat. Yes, we are told many times throughout the scriptures that Christ will also refine us. See Malachi 3:3, 3 Nephi 24:3, Doctrine & Covenants 128:24, and 1 Ne 20:10 for just a few examples. By definition, to refine precious metal, extreme heat is added in order to melt out the impurities. Christ actually orchestrates this refiner's fire not to melt us, but to purify us. The more we stand strong, the more our impurities can be removed from us.

The process of refining silver is very precarious indeed. The silversmith must sit and watch the silver the entire time it is in the flame, for the slightest overheating will ruin the precious metal.

The way the silversmith can tell when the silver is pure is simple: when he sees his image reflected in the precious metal. Doesn't this give you a whole new perspective on the scripture in Malachi 3:3, which tells us that Christ, will be the one sitting as the refiner. He is sitting there while the heat is on. He is watching over us. He is protecting us from the slightest degree of overheating. If we let Him, He will purify and perfect us. When He sees His image in our countenance... then we will be truly purified.

Chapter Six

Be the Chocolate Chip

There is a change that happens to us when we implement these four things: Through our covenants and commitments, we can enter into the gate. Then we hold on with all of our might, clinging to the iron rod each and every day. We keep our individuality, but fill our souls with integrity as we walk the path to personal perfection.

The changes may be so subtle that we can almost miss them on a day-to-day basis. But built over a period of time, as Bishop Burton states, we can "become so immersed in the Gospel of Jesus Christ that we become physically as well as mentally more and more like the Lord himself."[7]

We must offer up our whole souls to him, which is really the only thing that is truly ours to offer God. As we do this, an interesting change happens. We start to more fully live the Gospel; not because we are asked to, or forced to, but because we *want* to.

When we truly feel this change of heart, it no longer matters what others think, or even say about our choices. Bishop Burton declares that, "neither pressure nor force can be exerted upon us from outside..." when we have this change of heart it doesn't matter how hot the oven gets. We stand strong because of what we are internally, because of the changes and choices that we have made to follow and live the standards of the Gospel of Jesus Christ. "We then serve God in every way we can because we have been converted, our attitude has been changed and we now desire to become like Him both spiritually and physically."[7]

Christ is watching over us every step we take. Yes, it will get hot. Yes, it will be very unpleasant at times. He knows this. But with His help the heat will refine us. We will not melt. When we truly reflect the image of Him, our Savior Jesus Christ, in all that we say, all that we do, and all that we are, it is then that we will fully BE..... the chocolate chip.

Works Cited

1. Hales, Robert D. "The Covenant of Baptism: To Be in the Kingdom and Not of the Kingdom." *Ensign* Oct. 2000: 6-9.
2. Hinckley, Gordon B. "An Ensign to the Nations, a Light to the World." *Ensign* Nov. 2003: 82-85.
3. Faust, James E. "Devil's Throat." *Ensign* May 2003: 51-53.
4. Wirthlin, Joseph B. "Personal Integrity." *Ensign* May 1990: 30.
5. McKay, David O. "Unspotted from the World." *Ensign*, Aug. 2009: 24-29 (Excerpt from Oct. 1911 General Conference address.)
6. Dew, Sheri. *No One Can Take Your Place.* Salt Lake City:Deseret Book, 2004, Pg 11.
7. Burton, Theodore M. "The Need for Total Commitment." *Ensign* Jan 1974: 114.
8. Robinson, Stephen R. "Believing Christ." *Ensign* Apr. 1992: 5.